Significance
of a
Princess Warrior

A Scripture Study of Biblical Princess Warriors

by

Robyn S. Brinkley

Copyright © 2015 by Robyn S. Brinkley

Significance of a Princess Warrior
A Scripture Study of Biblical Princess Warriors
by Robyn S. Brinkley

First Printing, 2015

Printed in the United States of America

Edited by Xulon Press Publishing

ISBN 9781498434843

All rights reserved. This book or any portion thereof may not be reproduced or used in any manner whatsoever without the express written permission of the publisher except for the use of brief quotations in a book review.

Scripture quotations taken from the New International Version (NIV). Copyright © 1973, 1978, 1984, 2011 by Biblica, Inc.™. Used by permission. All rights reserved.

www.xulonpress.com

Contents

Week 1: *Introduction* 11

Week 2: Princess Warriors Are Meant for Companionship 17

Week 3: Princess Warriors Have Strength Together 33

Week 4: Princess Warriors Are Beautiful 43

Week 5: Princess Warriors Fight with Patience and Authority. 57

Week 6: Princess Warriors Give of Themselves 73

Week 7: Princess Warriors Manage Their Business. 89

Week 8: Princess Warriors Have
 a Statement of Significance . . 101
Week 9: Princess Warriors Are
 Proverbs 31 Women 109
Week 10: Conclusion and
 Celebration 125

Dedication

I am required to dedicate this, my first published writing, to my nephew Nathan Reynolds. All eleven of my nieces and nephews are precious children of God; but just like calling "shotgun," this nephew quietly requested that I dedicate my first work to him. You've got it, Nathan. And to the rest of my nieces and nephews—Savannah, Emma, Noah, Benjamin, Anna, Sally, Marie, Henry, Ruby and Joseph—I love you all and am thankful you are following Christ as your Savior! Your parents, grandparents—and aunt—are raising you as God has commanded.

Acknowledgments

As with any body of work, the number of people who help shape that body is numerous. To my affirmation partner, friend and person who first truly grasped God's mission through significance—Cari. Thank you for the hours spent monopolizing a booth at the local Panera, for listening to God's voice and for sharing the "chill bump" moments with me. Don't think you're off the hook—this is just the beginning!

Thank you to my dear friend Michelle, who has been like a sponge, listening and applying what we've learned together. You have been there through thick and thin, believing wholeheartedly and supporting this mission. It has been my pleasure to watch you grow and to have your growth spur me into more action for Princess Warriors. And to Heather not only for suggesting Michelle join one of my life groups years ago, but for being a dedicated, generous and loving friend I can trust with anything!

To my friends Holly and Terri—we will take this show on the road, Princess Warriors! We have fought much together, have tasted victory and have much more left to fight. Thank you for joining me in the battles over the past twenty years.

To the Princess Warriors who went through this curriculum and shared their hearts, their hurts and their victories— Monica, Carol, Nina, Waynette, Donna and

Acknowledgments

Stephanie—thank you for being vulnerable and willing!

To my family—thank you for bringing God into my life, supporting me in all I have done, picking me up in my failures and sharing in my victories! I love you!

Finally, to my son, Joshua—you are the light of my life. Words can never express how I feel about God bringing you into this world and allowing me the honor to be your mama. You are a remarkable man, and anything is possible for you as a warrior for Christ!

WEEK 1

Introduction

Significance of a Princess Warrior is an exploration of biblical Princess Warriors whose stories are not dissimilar to ours. God chose ordinary, seemingly unremarkable, even criminal women for His kingdom purpose. Each sought God, embraced her royal position and fulfilled her purpose.

Just like the Princess Warriors in this study, you and I are royalty. God has given us skills, tools and resources with which to fight for His kingdom. He clothes us with supernatural armor. His Word gives us the battle plan.

God is supreme commander, and we are His Princess Warriors.

To embrace our royalty, we must first acknowledge our significance. God created each and every one of us.

> For you created my inmost being; you knit me together in my mother's womb. I praise you because I am fearfully and wonderfully made; your works are wonderful, I know that full well (Psalm 139:13-14).

He knows everything about us, even the number of hairs on our heads.

> Are not two sparrows sold for a penny? Yet not one of them will fall to the ground outside your Father's care. And even the very hairs of your head are all numbered. So don't be

afraid; you are worth more than many sparrows (Matthew 10:29-31).

Still, we are human and become overwhelmed and fearful. Ever faithful, God provides His assurance.

Do not be afraid of them, the Lord your God himself will fight for you (Deuteronomy 3:22).

"Do not be afraid of them, for I am with you and will rescue you," declares the Lord (Jeremiah 1:8).

Don't be afraid; you are worth more than many sparrows (Matthew 10:31).

The Lord is my light and my salvation—whom shall I fear? The Lord is the stronghold of my life—of whom shall I be afraid? (Psalm 27:1).

The angel said to the women, "Do not be afraid, for I know that you are looking for Jesus, who was crucified" (Matthew 28:5).

But the angel said to her, "Do not be afraid, Mary; you have found favor with God" (Luke 1:30).

No matter our stage in life, we were created for a purpose. Life is full of peace and battles; happiness and sorrow; joyful times and melancholy moments. Whether we feel celebrated and revered, or unimportant, beat down and overlooked, we are significant. We are God's Princess Warriors, designed to worship Him and complete His plan.

Introduction

Whether this is your first Bible study or one of many, it is my prayer that at the conclusion you will take up your royal armor and truly believe

I am fearfully and wonderfully made. I am significant in Christ. I will fight the good fight as a Princess Warrior for the Lord.

If you are on this journey with part of a group, take this time to introduce yourselves, share why you feel compelled to join this study and spend some time learning about the other Princess Warriors in your group.

Thank you for taking this journey with me, Princess Warrior! Praise be to God alone.

Peace and Blessings!

Robyn S. Brinkley

WEEK 2

Princess Warriors Are Meant For Companionship

Welcome, Princess Warrior! God created each of us to be significant. He has given us numerous examples of significant women in both the Old and New Testaments.

We are called to be strong and courageous in our fight for our beliefs. As Princess Warriors, our roles are diverse. God has given us the capacity to be a wife, mother, sister, daughter, comforter, leader, businesswoman and Princess Warrior. Daily we fight for what matters most to us—what is significant.

We are called to fulfill so many responsibilities, but many women often feel beat down, tired, unimportant. Sometimes it seems the world wants *everything* we have to give and provides *nothing* for us in return. Certainly God's desire for us is more than the white picket fence, diaper changing, potluck organizing, high-heel wearing, boardroom dynamic female ninja so often portrayed in commercials and magazine advertisements. Whether you enjoy making jell-o molds and organizing potlucks or commanding a boardroom, all of these roles/responsibilities are important. But—and this is big—they are only *part* of what God created us to be.

Princess Warriors Are Meant For Companionship

God's desire is for us to be significant in *His* purpose. To use our skills, gifts and circumstances to further His kingdom, so that all of His children, warriors and Princess Warriors alike, experience eternal life with Him in heaven.

The first two weeks of our study will focus on how companionship and friendships matter. If you are participating in this study as a group, this will prayerfully be the beginning of some lasting friendships. It is vitally important to trust each other and be trusted. Open your hearts and minds to being vulnerable before fellow Princess Warriors and God. Love and be loved as Christ loves the church.

God does not desire us to be alone. He created us for companionship. The first example of this occurs in the very beginning of time. God created Adam, and shortly afterward He recognized Adam needed a suitable companion, a helper.

> The Lord God said, "It is not good for the man to be alone. I will make a helper suitable for him." Now the Lord God had formed out of the ground all the wild animals and all the birds in the sky. He brought them to the man to see what he would name them; and whatever the man called each living creature, that was its name. So the man gave names to all the livestock, the birds in the sky and all the wild animals. But for Adam no suitable helper was found. So the Lord God caused the man to fall into a deep sleep; and while he was sleeping, he took one of the man's ribs and then closed up the place with flesh. Then the Lord God made a woman from

the rib he had taken out of the man, and he brought her to the man. The man said,

> "This is now bone of my bones
> and flesh of my flesh;
> she shall be called 'woman,'
> for she was taken out of man"
> (Genesis 2:18-23, NIV).

We usually think of this Scripture passage as God creating a wife for Adam—which is true.

That is why a man leaves his father and mother and is united to his wife, and they become one flesh (Genesis 2:24).

But it is also represents that God recognized that His creation, man, is not as effective alone. We are made for companionship. We are created to help each other.

Jesus shares in the book of John:

As the Father has loved me, so have I loved you. Now remain in my love. If you keep my commands, you will remain in my love, just as I have kept my Father's commands and remain in his love. I have told you this so that my joy may be in you and that your joy may be complete. My command is this: Love each other as I have loved you. Greater love has no one than this: to lay down one's life for one's friends. You are my friends if you do what I command. I no longer call you servants, because a servant does not know his master's business. Instead, I have called you friends, for everything that I learned from my Father

I have made known to you. You did not choose me, but I chose you and appointed you so that you might go and bear fruit—fruit that will last— and so that whatever you ask in my name the Father will give you. This is my command: Love each other (John 15:9-17, NIV, emphasis added).

Solomon shares the importance of *godly* companionship.

Walk with the wise and become wise, for a companion of fools suffers harm (Proverbs 13:20, NIV).

As iron sharpens iron, so one person sharpens another (Proverbs 27:17, NIV).

Significance of a Princess Warrior

One example of Princess Warrior companionship is in the story of Mary and Elizabeth. While bound together as family, they were also trusted friends. Mary and Elizabeth were each favored by God and would give birth to boys who would change the world—Mary would deliver Jesus, and Elizabeth, John the Baptist.

> You will conceive and give birth to a son, and you are to call him Jesus. He will be great and will be called the Son of the Most High. The Lord God will give him the throne of his father David, and he will reign over Jacob's descendants forever; his kingdom will never end (Luke 1:31-33, NIV).

> Even Elizabeth your relative is going to have a child in her old age, and she who was said to be unable to conceive

is in her sixth month. For no word from God will ever fail (Luke 1:36-37, NIV).

What was Mary to do? News of this magnitude had to be shared with someone who would understand. If you were Mary, would you be apprehensive? Who would believe her? Still a virgin, but pregnant with the Son of God?

At that time Mary got ready and hurried to a town in the hill country of Judea, where she entered Zechariah's home and greeted Elizabeth (Luke 1:39-40, NIV).

Mary had to choose carefully with whom she would share the exciting yet terrifying news. Cousins by marriage, separated by miles and of different generations, Mary and

Elizabeth were still close enough in love and friendship that Mary rushed to tell Elizabeth the exciting news. She knew Elizabeth would understand. God ordained their friendship, and upon entering each other's presence both Princess Warriors were rewarded.

> When Elizabeth heard Mary's greeting, the baby leaped in her womb, and Elizabeth was filled with the Holy Spirit. In a loud voice she exclaimed: "Blessed are you among women, and blessed is the child you will bear! But why am I so favored, that the mother of my Lord should come to me? As soon as the sound of your greeting reached my ears, the baby in my womb leaped for joy. Blessed is she who has believed that the Lord would fulfill his promises to her!" (Luke 1:41-45, NIV).

Princess Warriors Are Meant For Companionship

God created us for companionship, both with godly people on this earth and with God Himself. Seek His direction as you enter into discussion.

DISCUSSION

1. In today's world what would the conversation between Mary and Elizabeth sound like? (Review Luke 1:41-56.)
2. Do you have a friend like Elizabeth with whom you can share your most intimate feelings?
3. Discuss what being a friend means to you. What do you expect of your true friends? Be specific—real actions, feelings.

    (ex: A true friend answers my calls/texts immediately, or at least as soon as they are out of their coma because that's the

only reason they don't answer on the first ring; a true friend shows up on my doorstep with creamy potato soup when I am sick.)
4. Are you the type of friend you expect others to be?
5. How do your expectations compare to John 15:9-17?

On our journey to becoming Princess Warriors, you must become vulnerable and share your heart with your fellow Princess Warriors. You must learn to trust. . .and be trusted.

Everything shared in this group should be kept within this group. If there is ever a concern with another Princess Warrior, I invite your group to follow Jesus' model in Matthew 18:15-17.

> If your brother or sister sins, go and point out their fault, just between

the two of you. If they listen to you, you have won them over. But if they will not listen, take one or two others along, so that "every matter may be established by the testimony of two or three witnesses." If they still refuse to listen, tell it to the church; and if they refuse to listen even to the church, treat them as you would a pagan or a tax collector (Matthew 18:15-17, NIV).

HOMEWORK

During your prayer time this week review John 15:9-17, especially verses 12-14. Pray about your friendships. Who are those you can trust? How can you be a trustworthy friend?

My command is this: Love each other as I have loved you. Greater love has no one than this: to lay down one's life for one's friends. You are my friends if you do what I command (John 15:12-14, NIV).

Statement of Significance—Introduction

Throughout the first seven weeks each Princess Warrior will be encouraged to create a statement of significance as part of your homework. (A statement of significance is also known as a testimony.) Whether you already have a statement of significance or not does not matter. Your journey to becoming a Princess Warrior will prayerfully change who and what you are as a believer in Jesus Christ.

You Are Significant to Christ!

Princess Warriors Are Meant For Companionship

In creating your statement, use the following questions as a guide. Each week as part of your homework you will review what you answered the previous week and begin to form a powerful statement that represents your significance.

Week 1 Statement of Significance
(Be specific and honest.)

Review the following questions and answer as many as you can with as little or as much detail as you would like. This will be a work in progress over the next several weeks.

1. What was your life like before believing in Jesus Christ as the Son of God?
2. How/when did you become a believer?
3. Since the day you became a believer until week 1 of Princess Warriors:
    (a) How has your life in Christ made a difference?

(b) How has His forgiveness impacted you?

4. This will evolve through the next several weeks: Since going through Princess Warriors, how have your thoughts, attitudes and emotions changed? Share how Christ is meeting your needs and what a relationship with Him means to you now.

WEEK 3

Princess Warriors Have Strength Together

Last week we learned God created us for companionship—for friendship. He did not desire us to be alone. Together, Princess Warriors should seek wisdom, love one another and keep each other sharp through accountability.

> Greater love has no one than this: to lay down one's life for one's friends. You are my friends if you do what I

command. I no longer call you servants, because a servant does not know his master's business. Instead, I have called you friends, for everything that I learned from my Father I have made known to you. You did not choose me, but I chose you and appointed you so that you might go and bear fruit—fruit that will last—and so that whatever you ask in my name the Father will give you. This is my command: Love each other (John 15:13-17, NIV).

Walk with the wise and become wise, for a companion of fools suffers harm (Proverbs 13:20, NIV).

As iron sharpens iron, so one person sharpens another (Proverbs 27:17, NIV).

Princess Warriors Have Strength Together

This week we will look at two Princess Warriors with a strong bond—Ruth and Naomi. Ruth's story is so significant that she has her own book in the Bible. Ruth was a Moabite, married to one of Naomi's sons. Naomi suffered great loss when her husband and then both of her sons died, leaving her with daughters-in-law Ruth and Orpah.

Naomi originally relocated to Moab from Bethlehem, and her daughters-in-law were both Moabites. After the death of her husband and sons, Naomi planned to return alone to her family in Bethlehem, leaving Ruth and Orpah in Moab.

> Then Naomi said to her two daughters-in-law, "Go back, each of you, to your mother's home. May the Lord show you kindness, as you have shown kindness to your dead

husbands and to me. May the Lord grant that each of you will find rest in the home of another husband." Then she kissed them goodbye, and they wept aloud and said to her, "We will go back with you to your people." But Naomi said, "Return home, my daughters. Why would you come with me? Am I going to have any more sons, who could become your husbands? Return home, my daughters; I am too old to have another husband. Even if I thought there was still hope for me—even if I had a husband tonight and then gave birth to sons— would you wait until they grew up? Would you remain unmarried for them? No, my daughters. It is more bitter for me than for you, because the Lord's hand has turned against me!" (Ruth 1:8-13, NIV).

Princess Warriors Have Strength Together

Naomi and her daughters-in-law were family by marriage, but the bond Ruth felt with Naomi had become exceptionally strong. While Naomi was determined to return home alone, Ruth recognized that Naomi had something special. Ruth knew that, alone, neither Princess Warrior would be complete.

At this they wept aloud again. Then Orpah kissed her mother-in-law goodbye, but Ruth clung to her. "Look," said Naomi, "your sister-in-law is going back to her people and her gods. Go back with her." But Ruth replied, "Don't urge me to leave you or to turn back from you. Where you go I will go, and where you stay I will stay. Your people will be my people and your God my God. Where you die I will die, and there I will be buried. May the Lord deal with me, be it ever so severely, if even death separates you and me." When Naomi realized that Ruth was determined to go with her, she stopped urging her (Ruth 1:14-18, NIV).

Ruth left everything she knew, her childhood home, family and traditions, to be with the person she admired and loved most.

Ruth also turned away from her god, the "fish god" Chemosh. Chemosh is referred to as a "detestable god" in 1 Kings 11:7.

Naomi's faith was in Almighty God, and her love for her family evidenced her faith in the Lord.

Naomi's faith was so undeniable, even in the face of tremendous loss, that it compelled Ruth to turn away from the faith of her fathers and worship the one true God. Naomi had remarkable influence on Ruth, leading both women in the strength given to Princess Warriors who follow God.

Together, these Princess Warriors endured loss, adversity and near poverty; but because of their bond through faith God provided His blessings. Ruth became the mother of Obed, who was the father of Jesse, and Jesse the father of David—part of the lineage of Jesus Christ.

DISCUSSION

1. Naomi invested in Ruth because she was her mother-in-law, and through that investment these Princess Warriors developed a strong bond. What does it mean to "invest" in a friend? (Note: An investment usually means you desire to make something better.)

2. Do you have someone in your life who invests in you—that just by being around them you are becoming a better person?
3. Do you have someone in your life *you* invest in?
4. Is there an opportunity for you to be more intentional about "receiving" the investment and "giving" the investment?

As a part of Princess Warriors, it is important to be vulnerable and also forge relationships that will build each other up. Ruth essentially said, "I want what you have, Naomi," and followed Naomi to Bethlehem. To be a true Princess Warrior, you have to be willing to share what you have—your significance in Jesus Christ—with those around you.

Each of us individually can be strong. Some Princess Warriors have athletic or physical strength; some are mentally tough; others command a good balance of both. Because God created us for companionship, it stands to reason that Princess Warriors are significantly stronger when together.

> Two are better than one,
> because they have a good return for their labor:
> If either of them falls down,
> one can help the other up.
> But pity anyone who falls
> and has no one to help them up.
> Also, if two lie down together, they will keep warm.
> But how can one keep warm alone?
> Though one may be overpowered,
> two can defend themselves.
> A cord of three strands is not quickly broken (Ecclesiastes 4:9-12).

HOMEWORK

Read through the book of Ruth in the Bible.

Continue to work on your statement of significance. If you haven't already completed questions 1 and 2 of your statement of significance, be sure to do so this week. Begin contemplating question 3, which will "evolve" more over the next few weeks.

WEEK 4

Princess Warriors Are Beautiful

As we have already experienced, throughout His Word, God shares the story of many significant Princess Warriors. These Princess Warriors are important historically, but they are meant to be examples of what Princess Warriors can do when they recognize their God-given roles.

This week, our focus is on a Princess Warrior who used her significance as a beautiful *and* intelligent Princess Warrior to fight for her people. Esther's story is significant, and, just like Ruth, Esther has an entire book in the Bible telling her story.

Esther risked her life for that of her people. This week we will do a brief study of what she accomplished and why. The book of Esther in the Bible is rich, and this week we are barely touching the surface of God's lessons shared through Esther's experience.

In all accounts, Esther was what we in today's world would expect of a super model. The Bible describes her as having a "lovely figure" and being "beautiful."

> This young woman, who was also known as Esther, had a lovely figure and was beautiful (Esther 2:7b, NIV).

King Xerxes was looking for a new wife. The search was something like America's Next Top Model—women from all over the realm applied, and the field was narrowed to a few lucky contestants. These contestants received special spa treatments, were taught how to act and serve, and were then presented to the king for his approval.

Before a young woman's turn came to go in to King Xerxes, she had to complete twelve months of beauty treatments prescribed for the women, six months with oil of myrrh and six with perfumes and cosmetics (Esther 2:12, NIV).

Imagine receiving spa and beauty treatments, free of charge, for a full year? What woman wouldn't appreciate that? But there was a catch. These spa and beauty treatments were necessary to make all of the chosen women *more* beautiful. The whole purpose was to be pleasing to the king.

While culture has changed since Esther's time, the emphasis on beauty and related feelings of inadequacy have continued. Esther's outer beauty, while pleasing to the king and finding her favor, still wasn't sufficient to make her queen. She was subjected to intensive intervention to meet the king's inflated expectations.

Let's pause here and ask a few questions for discussion.

1. How do you think Esther felt when she learned she made the first cut but wasn't aesthetically pleasing enough without help?
2. Esther "beautified" herself to please King Xerxes. Whom do you hope to please with your outward appearance?

Esther became queen, and her significance in God's kingdom started to reveal itself. Esther was of Jewish descent, adopted by her relative Mordecai who was an attendant in the citadel (the inner gate). She was a foreigner and kept her Jewish heritage a secret.

As a Jew, Mordecai refused to bow down to Haman, one of the king's noble men. Haman was a proud man, and Mordecai's refusal infuriated him. As Haman's anger grew, he began to despise all of the Jewish people scattered throughout the kingdom. Haman convinced the king that the Jews did not obey the king's laws and, therefore, should be killed.

Mordecai sent word to his relative, Queen Esther, to ask that she seek mercy from the king.

> For if you remain silent at this time, relief and deliverance for the Jews will arise from another place, but you and your father's family will perish. And who knows but that you have come

to your royal position for such a time as this? (Esther 4:14, NIV).

Think about how strong those words were: **"And who knows but that you have come to your royal position for such a time as this?"**

What Mordecai didn't know is that, while Esther worked hard to become queen, the king soon seemed to tire of her. For her to see the king she must be summoned, and she hadn't been called to see him for thirty days.

> All the king's officials and the people of the royal provinces know that for any man or woman who approaches the king in the inner court without being summoned the king has but one law: that they be put to death unless the king extends the gold scepter to them

and spares their lives. But thirty days have passed since I was called to go to the king (Esther 4:11, NIV).

To save her people, Esther's beauty was no longer enough; she would have to devise an intricate plan and use her position as queen. Seemingly having been rejected by King Xerxes, Esther would risk her very life to gain entry to the king's court. She put aside the rejection, changed her focus and embraced her role as a Princess Warrior.

So the king and Haman went to Queen Esther's banquet, and as they were drinking wine on the second day, the king again asked, "Queen Esther, what is your petition? It will be given you. What is your request? Even up to half the kingdom, it will be granted." Then Queen Esther answered, "If I have found favor with you, Your Majesty, and if it pleases you, grant me my life—this is my petition. And spare my people—this is my request. For I and my people have been sold to be destroyed, killed and annihilated. If we had merely been sold as male and female slaves, I would have kept quiet, because no such distress would justify disturbing the king." King Xerxes asked Queen Esther, "Who is he? Where is he— the man who has dared to do such a thing?" Esther said, "An adversary and enemy! This vile Haman!" Then Haman was terrified before the king and queen (Esther 7:1-6, NIV).

The evil that Haman intended was turned against him because Esther was bold enough to bring the fate of her people into the king's court. *She gained favor because of her beauty, but her significance was revealed when she fought for her people.*

> And who knows but that you have come to your royal position for such a time as this? (Esther 4:14, NIV).

DISCUSSION

1. How much time do you spend focusing on how you look, your outward beauty?
2. Do you feel that your focus is more on your outward appearance or on what God has created you to be from the inside out?
3. How can we change our focus, or the focus of those around us, so it

becomes our significance in Christ instead of our outward appearance?

4. As a Princess Warrior, you are royalty. Esther 4:14b says, "And who knows but that you have come to your royal position for such a time as this?" What is God telling you to use *your* royal position for at this significant time?

HOMEWORK

As you dry or curl your hair, put on your makeup, get dressed every single day this week—turn your thoughts toward God and how He sees you. When you look in the mirror recite the following words, either out loud or in your heart:

I am fearfully and wonderfully made.
I am significant!

Review the Scripture verses below. Haman was a man of this world, choosing to serve himself. Esther was fitted with the armor of God through faith. We will begin showing examples of the elements of armor next week. But think about what the below verses means to you. As you dress each day, are you wearing God's armor?

Finally, be strong in the Lord and in his mighty power. Put on the full armor of God, so that you can take your stand against the devil's schemes. For our struggle is not against flesh and blood, but against the rulers, against the authorities, against the powers of this dark world and against the spiritual forces of evil in the heavenly realms (Ephesians 6:10-12).

Continue working on your statement of significance.

You likely have at least a "draft" of answers to item 3. Finalize this and begin praying about God's desire for you over the course of Princess Warriors. We will share our statements of significance in a few weeks, and we pray your answers to item 4 will be revealed over the next three weeks.

1. What was your life like before believing in Jesus Christ as the Son of God?
2. How/when did you become a believer?
3. Since the day you became a believer until week 1 of Princess Warriors:
    (a) How has your life in Christ made a difference?
    (b) How has His forgiveness impacted you?
4. Since becoming a Princess Warrior, how have your thoughts, attitudes and emotions changed? Share how

Christ is meeting your needs and what a relationship with Him means to you now.

WEEK 5

Princess Warriors Fight With Patience And Authority

In this the twenty-first century, we have become impatient. We are an "instant gratification" society—from instant computer downloads of our favorite songs, movies, books, jokes and pictures, to our "fast food" restaurants. We expect "life" to be delivered quickly and without waiting. As Princess Warriors for God, we need to learn the art of patience. With patience we hear from God, and we can fight for what's right.

I wait for the Lord, my whole being waits, and in his word I put my hope (Psalm 130:5, NIV).

Throughout biblical history God's chosen have waited, some more patiently than others, until God raised up His "chosen human" to deliver His promises. Notice how I used the words "chosen human." This is because sometimes the "chosen human" was a warrior, and other times it was a Princess Warrior. Whether God's "chosen human" was male or female, he/she fought for what's right—for God's kingdom.

This week we look at the account of Deborah and Jael. Deborah was a married woman in high regard as a judge, a prophet and a leader. As judge, Deborah held court to decide disputes between the people. As a leader, she assessed security threats and directed Israel's army.

> Now Deborah, a prophet, the wife of Lappidoth, was leading Israel at that time. She held court under the Palm of Deborah between Ramah and Bethel in the hill country of Ephraim, and the Israelites went up to her to have their disputes decided (Judges 4:4-5, NIV).

The Israelites had been sold to Jabin, king of Canaan, and had been oppressed by his commander Sisera for twenty years. They prayed to God for deliverance, and He provided a "chosen human," a Princess Warrior named Deborah.

Significance of a Princess Warrior

She [Deborah] sent for Barak son of Abinoam from Kedesh in Naphtali and said to him, "The Lord, the God of Israel, commands you: 'Go, take with you ten thousand men of Naphtali and Zebulun and lead them up to Mount Tabor. I will lead Sisera, the commander of Jabin's army, with his chariots and his troops to the Kishon River and give him into your hands." Barak said to her, "If you go with me, I will go; but if you don't go with me, I won't go" (Judges 4:6-8, NIV).

Deborah formulated a battle plan to deliver Israel out from under Jaban and Sisera's oppression. This plan included the commander Barak to lead an army of ten thousand men to defeat Sisera. Barak, a warrior, refused to lead his vast army to battle Sisera alone. Whether it was fear or disbelief in the battle plan, Barak refused his orders and would only proceed if Deborah, the Princess Warrior, fought by his side.

This is the opportunity for which Israel had been praying and waiting. Barak's training was for such a time as this. His orders were clear; yet he deferred the battle to Deborah.

Let's pause here and ask a few questions.

1. Why do you think Barak refused to fight Sisera without Deborah by his side?

2. What impact do you think twenty years of waiting had on Barak? on Deborah?

3. Why do you think Deborah appointed Barak? Do you think she was afraid; being respectful; being wise in her decision? Discuss.

Barak declined his role as leader. Instead of ordering Barak or another male commander to lead, Deborah's response was to lead the army to victory—a victory God would deliver into the hands of a woman, a Princess Warrior, instead of Barak.

"Certainly I will go with you," said Deborah. "But because of the course you are taking, the honor will not be yours, for the Lord will deliver Sisera into the hands of a woman." So Deborah went with Barak to Kedesh (Judges 4:9-10, NIV).

Sisera summoned from Harosheth Haggoyim to the Kishon River all his men and his nine hundred chariots fitted with iron.Then Deborah said to Barak, "Go! This is the day the Lord has given Sisera into your hands. Has not the Lord gone ahead of you?" So Barak went down Mount Tabor, with ten thousand men following him. At Barak's advance, the Lord routed Sisera and all his chariots and army by the sword, and Sisera got down from his chariot and fled on foot. Barak pursued the chariots and army as far as Harosheth Haggoyim, and all Sisera's troops fell by the sword; not a man was left (Judges 4:13-16, NIV).

Deborah knew whose victory this truly was—God's—and she had to remind Barak: "Go! This is the day the Lord has given Sisera into your hands. Has not the Lord gone ahead of you?" Barak didn't trust himself to lead the army because he didn't trust God to deliver. Deborah, on the other hand, knew that as the "chosen human," the Princess Warrior, she was already clothed with the armor of God and that God was leading and would deliver His people out of the misery of Sisera's oppression.

The battle continues as Sisera fled from the battlefield. Earlier I mentioned Jael. Deborah was not the only Princess Warrior victorious in this account. Jael's husband was in alliance with Sisera's king, Jabin. Although her husband's allegiance was with Sisera, Jael's allegiance was to God.

> Sisera, meanwhile, fled on foot to the tent of Jael, the wife of Heber the Kenite, because there was an alliance between Jabin king of Hazor and the family of Heber the Kenite. Jael went out to meet Sisera and said to him, "Come, my lord; come right in. Don't be afraid." So he entered her tent, and she covered him with a blanket. "I'm thirsty," he said. "Please give me some

water." She opened a skin of milk, gave him a drink and covered him up. "Stand in the doorway of the tent," he told her. "If someone comes by and asks you, 'Is anyone in there?' say 'No.' "But Jael, Heber's wife, picked up a tent peg and a hammer and went quietly to him while he lay fast asleep, exhausted. She drove the peg through his temple into the ground, and he died. Just then Barak came by in pursuit of Sisera, and Jael went out to meet him. "Come," she said, "I will show you the man you're looking for." So he went in with her, and there lay Sisera with the tent peg through his temple—dead. On that day God subdued Jabin king of Canaan before the Israelites. And the hand of the Israelites pressed harder and harder against Jabin king of Canaan until they destroyed him (Judges 4:17-24, NIV).

God created a Princess Warrior in Jael, and she defeated the army commander Sisera single-handedly by luring him into her tent and driving a tent peg through his temple. Think of the mental and physical strength Jael exhibited to drive a tent peg through Sisera's skull, strength that could only have come from God Himself.

The war was waged and battle won by two Princess Warriors. They believed in God's strategy, were clothed in His armor and experienced victory!

As believers in Christ, we are all victors. We wage battles every single day. We decide disputes, confront our enemies and command armies. Sometimes we exercise patience, sometimes not, but God always delivers us as long as we are wearing His armor and seeking His allegiance.

Before we go into further discussion, let's look at what it means to wear God's armor.

Finally, be strong in the Lord and in his mighty power. Put on the full armor of God, so that you can take your stand against the devil's schemes. For our struggle is not against flesh and blood, but against the rulers, against the authorities, against the powers of this dark world and against the spiritual forces of evil in the heavenly realms.

Therefore put on the full armor of God, so that when the day of evil comes, you may be able to stand your ground, and after you have done everything, to stand. Stand firm then, with the belt of truth buckled around your waist, with the breastplate of righteousness in place, and with your feet fitted with the readiness that comes from the gospel of peace. In addition to all this, take up the shield of faith, with which you can extinguish all the flaming arrows of the evil one. Take the helmet of salvation and the sword of the Spirit, which is the word of God (Ephesians 6:10-17, NIV, emphasis added).

As we discuss the next few questions, think about the armor.

Belt of truth

Breastplate of righteousness

Feet fitted with the readiness of the gospel of peace

Shield of faith

Helmet of salvation

Sword of the Spirit. which is the Word of God

1. What does it mean to be clothed with the armor of God?
2. Do you feel Barak was wearing God's armor? If not, which piece(s) was he missing?
3. Give some examples of battles we fight and disputes we decide today.
4. Israel waited twenty years for this battle. Give examples of something you are waiting on and how God is teaching you patience.

In considering patience, God has used David's words more times than I can count as a reminder that, in His timing, He will deliver. Together God and the Princess Warrior in me will rise victorious.

I waited patiently for the Lord;
he turned to me and heard my cry.

He lifted me out of the slimy pit,
out of the mud and mire;
he set my feet on a rock
and gave me a firm place to stand.
He put a new song in my mouth,
a hymn of praise to our God.
Many will see and fear the Lord
and put their trust in him (Psalm 40:1-3, NIV).

Princess Warrior, we were created to fight for what's right! Although our desire may be for a warrior to take the lead, sometimes it's up to us to wage war, lead the troops and take up our armor to defeat our enemies. Some of our battlefields are in boardrooms, on playgrounds and in our homes (and I'm sure we can all agree the big box grocery store is a huge war zone. . .but that's a story for another time). No matter which battlefield we face, as Princess Warriors we will remember:

We are fearfully and wonderfully made. We are significant in Christ. We will fight the good fight as Princess Warriors for the Lord!

HOMEWORK

1. Put on your armor daily. Recite Ephesians 6:10-17, stating "I" and "my" for "we" and "our."
2. Continue your statement of significance. I hope you are beginning to see a bit of Ruth, Esther, Deborah and/or Jael in yourself. You are learning how to wear your armor and may be seeing some changes in your relationship with the one true living God,

through Christ Jesus, our Savior. Ask God how you can use His examples of biblical Princess Warriors to bring yourself in closer relationship with Him.

Princess Warrior, wear your armor proudly and seriously because the enemy is real! Just as Deborah wore physical armor in battle, we must wear supernatural armor!

WEEK 6

Princess Warriors Give Of Themselves

Princess Warrior, we have clothed ourselves with the armor of God and are starting to see God has given us just the right gifts to fight for His kingdom. We have learned the power of friendship, that we are all beautiful and that as Princess Warriors we fight for what's right. This week we are going to see how, in our fight for God's kingdom living, we are willing to risk so we can give what we have.

First, let's look at a "sinful woman" in Luke chapter 7. At the end of the chapter, Scripture tells us Jesus attended dinner at a Pharisee's home. There he met a sinful woman (in other accounts we learn this is Mary Magdalene). She stood behind Jesus and wept, her tears falling upon his feet. She dried his tear-laden feet with her hair and then anointed his feet with perfume.

When one of the Pharisees invited Jesus to have dinner with him, he went to the Pharisee's house and reclined at the table. A woman in that town who lived a sinful life learned that Jesus was eating at the Pharisee's house, so she came there with an alabaster jar of perfume. As she stood behind him at his feet weeping, she began to wet his feet with her tears. Then she wiped them with her hair, kissed them and poured perfume on them. When the Pharisee who had invited him saw this, he said to himself, "If this man were a prophet, he would know who is touching him and what kind of woman she is—that she is a sinner (Luke 7:36-39, NIV).

Then he turned toward the woman and said to Simon, "Do you see this woman? I came into your house. You did not give me any water for my feet, but she wet my feet with her tears and wiped them with her hair. You did not give me a kiss, but this woman, from the time I entered, has not stopped kissing my feet. You did not put oil on my head, but she has poured perfume on my feet. Therefore, I tell you, her many sins have been forgiven—as her great love has shown. But whoever has been forgiven little loves little."

Then Jesus said to her, "Your sins are forgiven."

The other guests began to say among themselves, "Who is this who even forgives sins?"

Jesus said to the woman, "Your faith has saved you; go in peace" (Luke 7:44-50, NIV).

It appears everyone around town was aware of the sins committed by this Princess Warrior. Even so, she risked humiliation by entering the Pharisee's home to present perfume to Jesus. She risked much and gave what she had and received in return the ultimate gift—forgiveness.

Mary Magdalene (the "sinful woman") is a well-studied Princess Warrior in the New Testament. She was not one of the "twelve" (male disciples) but was a disciple of Jesus Christ alongside her male and female counterparts. While Mary Magdalene is referenced many times throughout the Gospels, several other Princess Warriors, including Joanna and Susanna, accompanied her. We will pick up the story right where we left off.

After this, Jesus traveled about from one town and village to another, proclaiming the good news of the kingdom of God. The Twelve were with him, and also some women who had been cured of evil spirits and diseases: Mary (called Magdalene) from whom seven demons had come out;

Joanna the wife of Chuza, the manager of Herod's household; Susanna; and many others. These women [Princess Warriors] were helping to support them out of their own means (Luke 8:1-3, NIV).

The key verse here is the third.

Joanna the wife of Chuza, the manager of Herod's household; Susanna; and many others. These women were helping to support them out of their own means.

Five things stand out to me.
- Because of their faith, Mary Magdalene, Joanna and Susanna had all been cured of evil spirits and/or diseases;

Princess Warriors Give Of Themselves

- These Princess Warriors likely had some level of financial means;
- They gave of their finances and of themselves in support of the Messiah;
- They walked alongside the warriors, as disciples; and
- They all put their own lives at risk (warrior and Princess Warrior alike), but Joanna with a higher degree of risk, since her husband managed Herod's household (Herod being the very man who would mock Jesus and return him to Pilate, ultimately resulting in his crucifixion).

These three Princess Warriors found favor with Jesus, demonstrated faith and were cured of evil spirits and/or illnesses. Defying religious leaders and King Herod, and at risk of persecution, they became devoted followers.

Joanna's level of risk was compounded by the fact that she was the wife of Chuza, who attended to all of Herod's household finances and responsibilities. While this position gave Joanna opportunity to share the gospel in circles the male disciples could not attain, this made her even more vulnerable.

All disciples placed themselves in jeopardy of persecution. And while all disciples made substantial sacrifice (family, job and so on), financial sacrifice to support the ministry is credited to Princess Warriors Mary Magdalene, Joanna, Susanna and "many others."

In a time when women were not very well regarded, here is an account of Princess Warriors who provided financial support for the very man who would later be crucified as a criminal.

Princess Warriors Give Of Themselves

The Princess Warriors in Luke 8 gave of what they had so they could hear these words:

Jesus said to the woman, "Your faith has saved you; go in peace" (Luke 7:50).

I want to share a bit more information about these Princess Warriors, but first let's answer some questions.

DISCUSSION

1. We are all like the "sinful woman." We approach Jesus from the place of a broken heart. Whether we recognize it or not, when we approached Jesus for the first time, we were weeping in some way or another. While the weeping by the sinful woman was true

tears dropping to the feet of Jesus, talk about the kind of "weeping" you may have experienced that brought you to His feet.

2. All of the Princess Warriors discussed this week risked much to receive forgiveness and healing and to become Christ followers. Have you faced a time when you had to step out on a limb and risk something for your faith? Please explain.

3. The Princess Warriors in Luke 8 are the only people credited in the New Testament with financially supporting the ministry of Christ. Often, a family may tithe as a family unit. Whether or not you participate in the biblical tithe, what are you doing/can you do to support Christ and His church? (This does not have to be monetary.)

4. The Bible generally focuses on warriors (men), so when Princess Warriors are mentioned, it can be assumed they were significant. What are we, as twenty-first century Princess Warriors, doing to make sure we are significant in Christ?

Last, it is important to share that Mary Magdalene, Joanna and Susanna stayed with Jesus, even through to the end. They were all witnesses to the brutal crucifixion and mourned with the eleven remaining disciples. They had the honor of witnessing at least one more miracle.

Jesus Has Risen

> On the first day of the week, very early in the morning, the women took the spices they had prepared and went to the tomb. They found the stone rolled

away from the tomb, but when they entered, they did not find the body of the Lord Jesus. While they were wondering about this, suddenly two men in clothes that gleamed like lightning stood beside them. In their fright the women bowed down with their faces to the ground, but the men said to them, "Why do you look for the living among the dead? He is not here; he has risen! Remember how he told you, while he was still with you in Galilee: 'The Son of Man must be delivered over to the hands of sinners, be crucified and on the third day be raised again.'" Then they remembered his words.

When they came back from the tomb, they told all these things to the Eleven and to all the others. It was Mary Magdalene, Joanna, Mary the mother of James, and the others with them who told this to the apostles. But they did not believe the women, because their words seemed to them like nonsense. Peter, however, got up and ran to the tomb. Bending over, he saw the strips of linen lying by themselves, and he went away, wondering to himself what had happened (Luke 24:1-12, NIV).

As Princess Warriors, we must fight for what's right, give of what we have and stick with it until the end. God has one more miracle up His sleeve—the miracle of eternal life!

Are you beginning to feel like a Princess Warrior? Discuss why or why not and remember:

We are fearfully and wonderfully made. We are significant in Christ. We will fight the good fight as Princess Warriors for the Lord.

HOMEWORK

This week focus on our core statement, substituting the word *We* with the word *I*.

I am fearfully and wonderfully made. I am significant in Christ. I will fight the good fight as a Princess Warrior for the Lord.

1. How are you doing on your statement of significance? If you need help, reach out to your leader; she is more than willing to assist! For those who are willing, we will be sharing our statements of significance in our group in **two** weeks.

Jesus said to the woman,

> "Your faith has saved you; go in peace" (Luke 7:50).

Walk in peace, Princess Warrior!

WEEK 7

Princess Warriors Manage Their Business

Princess Warrior, we have learned and shared much over the past several weeks. We know we are meant to develop strong friendships, we are beautiful, we fight for what's right and we give of ourselves. We have donned the armor of God and are called to fight the good fight. We are recognizing that we are fearfully and wonderfully made, and we are being built up so we can fight alongside our fellow warriors and Princess Warriors for the kingdom of God.

This week we are going to look at how we manage our own business by learning about a prudent businesswoman, Lydia.

Before we get too far into this lesson, let's define *business*.

> An occupation, *profession*, or trade (www.dictionary.com).

Profession is defined:

> A vocation requiring knowledge of some department of learning or science (www.dictionary.com).

Business is anything we do for a profession, a vocation—*anything that provides for our families or us.* As Princess Warriors, we may be outside-the-home business professionals or inside-the-home domestic engineers; either way, we all have business to tend.

This week's story is told from Paul's perspective, when he and Silas travel to Philippi. There they met many people, including Lydia, a dealer in purple cloth.

On the Sabbath we went outside the city gate to the river, where we expected to find a place of prayer. We sat down and began to speak to the women who had gathered there. One of those listening was a woman from the city of Thyatira named Lydia, a dealer in purple cloth. She was a worshiper of God. The Lord opened her heart to respond to Paul's message. When she and the members of her household were baptized, she invited us to her home. "If you consider me a believer in the Lord," she said, "come and stay at my house." And she persuaded us (Acts 16:13-15, NIV).

As we have been learning, women are a significant part of Christian history, just as in this account.

When Paul and Silas went outside the city gates to pray, they met Lydia together with a group of other Princess Warriors. We know from the text that Lydia's business was in selling purple cloth—which was usually purchased by those of wealth and/or prominence.

In a male-dominated culture, Lydia likely knew she had to employ every advantage possible to be successful. As with any good businessperson, her driving force was likely to provide for her and her family. Her initial business outline may have looked something like this:

- Set immediate and future goals to meet her (and her family's) needs;
- Stay flexible to meet those goals;
- Understand the market;
- Provide valuable products and services;
- Remain aware of competitors;
- Employ marketing strategies to beat competitors.

Lydia knew her product. She lived in an area where environmental factors contributed to excellent dye properties. She knew her market, as this area attracted people of wealth and prominence to purchase dyed cloth. And, most important, Lydia knew her ultimate supplier.

She was a worshiper of God (Acts 16:14, NIV).

Because Lydia was a faithful believer in our God, the Lord opened her heart to the message Paul and Silas were sharing—the Messiah had come, offering salvation to Jew and Gentile alike.

The Lord opened her heart to respond to Paul's message. When she and the members of her household were baptized, she invited us to her home. "If you consider me a believer in the Lord," she said, "come and stay at my house." And she persuaded us (Acts16:14b-15, NIV).

Lydia knew her business, and she knew her Savior. She and her household professed their faith publicly and followed in the symbolic act of baptism, just as Jesus instructed:

Therefore go and make disciples of all nations, baptizing them in the name of the Father and of the Son and of the Holy Spirit, and teaching them to obey everything I have commanded you. And surely I am with you always, to the very end of the age (Matthew 28:19-20).

Lydia tended to her business, which included caring for her entire household. She was a prudent businesswoman, ensuring that not only her outside business was successful, but also that the business inside her home would flourish. By including her household (family and servants) in hearing the salvation message, Lydia's household received the gift of eternal life.

DISCUSSION

1. Discuss the differences between an outside-the-home businessperson and an inside-the-home domestic engineer. What are some challenges each faces in leading those important to us to become believers?

2. Review and discuss each bullet point in the business outline above. Apply each bullet point to your business (outside the home, inside the home or both) and discuss.

3. Lydia was an example of an outside-the-home businessperson. How do you think this impacted her inside-the-home responsibilities? Were those responsibilities any different from those in the twentieth-first century?

4. Discuss how you tend to your business. Do you know your market, your product, and do you rely on God?

Princess Warrior, Lydia's husband was not mentioned in this Scripture passage, but assuming she was married she led her husband and her entire household as a godly woman. Even though she was an outside-the-home businessperson, she conducted her business and her home in a way that pleased the Lord (and caused Him to open her heart for salvation).

> Wives, in the same way submit yourselves to your own husbands so that, *if any of them do not believe the word, they may be won over without words by the behavior of their wives, when they see the purity and reverence of your lives* (1 Peter 3:1-2, NIV, emphasis added).

At great risk of persecution—the least of which would be to lose her business—Lydia (with the approval of her household) invited Paul and Silas to stay with her again after they had been jailed and released.

She understood her risks—she was an astute businesswoman. But more than that, she was a significant Princess Warrior.

After Paul and Silas came out of the prison, they went to Lydia's house, where they met with the brothers and sisters and encouraged them. Then they left (Acts 16:40, NIV).

HOMEWORK

Princess Warrior, next week we will be sharing our statements of significance. Are you ready? Do not be afraid. No story is too simple or too difficult to be shared with our Princess Warriors. Put on your armor and remember:

> We are fearfully and wonderfully made. We are significant in Christ. We will fight the good fight as Princess Warriors for the Lord!

WEEK 8

Princess Warriors Have A Statement Of Significance

Princess Warrior, you are significant! From the day you were conceived, God already planned the number of hairs on your head:

> And even the very hairs of your head are all numbered (Matthew 10:30, NIV).

We are all sinful beings; no sin is greater or lesser than any other. Every Princess Warrior going through this journey with you is a sinner. And every Princess Warrior and warrior alike are significant enough that God desires that we join Him in heaven.

Because God cared so much for each of us, He sent His Son, Jesus Christ, to this earth. By Christ's life, death and resurrection you, Princess Warrior, have the opportunity for eternal life in heaven.

> For God so loved the world that he gave his one and only Son, that whoever believes in him shall not perish but have eternal life (John 3:16, NIV).

Jesus' words were shared throughout the Gospels.

Jesus answered, "I am the way and the truth and the life. No one comes to the Father except through me" (John 14:6, NIV).

Paul let us know it was as simple as believing in our hearts and professing with our mouths that Jesus Christ is Lord.

If you declare with your mouth, "Jesus is Lord," and believe in your heart that God raised him from the dead, you will be saved. For it is with your heart that you believe and are justified, and it is with your mouth that you profess your faith and are saved (Romans 10:9-10, NIV).

Princess Warrior, because of your significance Jesus Himself declared that He is preparing a place just for you where you will join Him in eternity.

> And if I go and prepare a place for you, I will come back and take you to be with me that you also may be where I am (John 14:3).

How glorious will that day be? How glorious is today? This is the day you will share your statement of significance with your fellow Princess Warriors. Whether you've shared many times in your life, or never shared before, today will be significant because you recognize yourself as a Princess Warrior for Christ.

Take a deep breath. Focus on Christ. Share with your heart. Your story is HIStory and is significant!

As a reminder, here is a basic outline of what you will be sharing.

1. What was your life like before believing in Jesus Christ as the Son of God?
2. How/when did you become a believer?
3. Since the day you became a believer until week 1 of Princess Warriors:
    (a) How has your life in Christ made a difference?
    (b) How has His forgiveness impacted you?
4. Since joining Princess Warriors, how have your thoughts, attitudes and emotions changed? Share how Christ is meeting your needs and what a relationship with Him means to you now.

We are fearfully and wonderfully made. We are significant in Christ. We will fight the good fight as Princess Warriors for the Lord!

HOMEWORK

1. Remember your armor:

Finally, be strong in the Lord and in his mighty power. Put on the full armor of God, so that you can take your stand against the devil's schemes. For our struggle is not against flesh and blood, but against the rulers, against the authorities, against the powers of this dark world and against the spiritual forces of evil in the heavenly realms.

> *Therefore put on the full armor of God, so that when the day of evil comes, you may be able to stand your ground, and after you have done everything, to stand. Stand firm then, with the belt of truth buckled around your waist, with the breastplate of righteousness in place, and with your feet fitted with the readiness that comes from the gospel of peace. In addition to all this, take up*

the shield of faith, with which you can extinguish all the flaming arrows of the evil one. Take the helmet of salvation and the sword of the Spirit, which is the word of God (Ephesians 6:10-17, NIV, emphasis added).

2. Read through Proverbs 31. Are you a Proverbs 31 woman? Do you live up to every characteristic? Let me ask you this: Do you ever break any of the ten commandments? While the character of a Proverbs 31 woman is something we should all strive for, we are also covered by grace. Next week let's explore how a Princess Warrior looks at Proverbs 31, how we fight for significance in our journey, how we support the warriors in our lives and how we leave a legacy for our families.

WEEK 9

Princess Warriors Are Proverbs 31 Women

Princess Warrior, we have learned and shared much over the past weeks. I pray you are feeling more and more significant in Christ. This week we are going to learn how we can truly be Proverbs 31 Princess Warriors.

Proverbs 31 is often used as a guideline for how a Christian woman should live. It is often touted as the standard, or trademark, of a virtuous woman—a bar that all Christian women should strive to reach.

As you read the Scripture passage, think about women you know. Is there anyone who truly fits every verse in this passage?

Proverbs 31:10 A wife of noble character who can find? She is worth far more than rubies.

11 Her husband has full confidence in her and lacks nothing of value.

12 She brings him good, not harm, all the days of her life.

13 She selects wool and flax and works with eager hands.

14 She is like the merchant ships, bringing her food from afar.

15 She gets up while it is still night; she provides food for her family and portions for her female servants.

16 She considers a field and buys it; out of her earnings she plants a vineyard.

17 She sets about her work vigorously; her arms are strong for her tasks.

18 She sees that her trading is profitable, and her lamp does not go out at night.

19 In her hand she holds the distaff and grasps the spindle with her fingers.

20 She opens her arms to the poor and extends her hands to the needy.

21 When it snows, she has no fear for her household; for all of them are clothed in scarlet.

22 She makes coverings for her bed; she is clothed in fine linen and purple.

23 Her husband is respected at the city gate, where he takes his seat among the elders of the land.

24 She makes linen garments and sells them, and supplies the merchants with sashes.

25 She is clothed with strength and dignity; she can laugh at the days to come.

26 She speaks with wisdom, and faithful instruction is on her tongue.

27 She watches over the affairs of her household and does not eat the bread of idleness.

28 Her children arise and call her blessed; her husband also, and he praises her:

29 "Many women do noble things, but you surpass them all."

30 Charm is deceptive, and beauty is fleeting; but a woman who fears the Lord is to be praised.

31 Honor her for all that her hands have done, and let her works bring her praise at the city gate.

DISCUSSION

1. What was your original perception of the Proverbs 31 Princess Warrior the first time you read this chapter?
2. Do you know any Proverbs 31 Princess Warriors? If so, who are they in your life, and what Proverbs 31 traits do they embody?

Like me, you may feel that being a Proverbs 31 Princess Warrior is very honorable, but overwhelming; desirable, but unattainable. For me, I felt as if I had failed before I even began trying to live up to these standards.

I believe God has a different idea for us, maybe something like this:

Stop comparing. Be you. Use the gifts God has granted to be the best "you" that you can be.

In our studies we have reviewed several Princess Warriors throughout biblical history. Each one was the best they could be with the gifts they were given. We do not know everything about each of these Princess Warriors. We know they were significant, and their stories clearly reflect several but not all of the attributes of a Proverbs 31 Princess Warrior.

Let's take a look at how they met the standards provided in this Scripture passage.

Mary and Elizabeth

Mary and Elizabeth were both pregnant with boys who would change the world. Elizabeth had been barren, unable to have a child, and the Lord prepared her body to conceive and give birth to John the Baptist. John would prepare the way for Christ's ministry.

Mary was young and had never been with a man. She became pregnant by the Lord God and gave birth to Jesus Christ, the Savior of the world.

Both Princess Warriors had much to boast about, and certainly Mary's story could top Elizabeth's if they were to be in competition. But they weren't; they were actually in communion. They both knew God was using them for His glory.

Their husbands and their children revered their mothers, recognizing them as important figures in their lives.

As Proverbs 31 Princess Warriors, they fulfilled this verse (among others):

Her children arise and call her blessed; her husband also, and he praises her: "Many women do noble things, but you surpass them all" (vv. 28-29).

Ruth and Naomi

Even though her husband had died, Ruth stayed with her mother-in-law, Naomi, as an act of honor and support. Ruth accepted Naomi's God and family as her own, and Ruth in turn was accepted as well. After reaching Naomi's homeland, Ruth sought work to support herself and her mother-in-law. What resulted was Ruth finding favor with Boaz and becoming part of the lineage of Jesus Christ Himself.

As a Proverbs 31 Princess Warrior, Ruth fulfilled these verses:

She selects wool and flax and works with eager hands (v. 13).

She sets about her work vigorously; her arms are strong for her tasks (v. 17).

Esther

King Xerxes chose Esther to become his queen because of her beauty. She gained her husband's respect and utilized her gifts to keep the Jewish people within the realm from destruction under the manipulation of Haman, the king's valued servant.

As a Proverbs 31 Princess Warrior, Esther fulfilled these verses:

Her husband has full confidence in her and lacks nothing of value (v. 11).

She brings him good, not harm, all the days of her life (v. 12).

Deborah and Jael

Deborah was a prophetess and a judge. She was extremely wise and spoke truth in a way that others recognized and followed her leadership. She devised a battle plan to defeat Sisera and lead her warriors into battle.

Jael, likewise, was wise, knowing this was God's battle to be won. When Sisera was delivered to her tent, she took his life by driving a tent peg through his skull and into the ground.

Obviously, both Princess Warriors were physically and mentally strong to become victorious in this battle. As Proverbs 31

Princess Warriors, Deborah and Jael fulfilled these verses:

> She is clothed with strength and dignity; she can laugh at the days to come (v. 25).

> She speaks with wisdom, and faithful instruction is on her tongue (v. 26).

Joanna, Susanna and Mary Magdalene

These three Princess Warriors were noted disciples of Jesus Christ. They are the only people referenced to have supported the ministry financially. They were financially astute and had a heart for the mission field. With their finances they planted a "vineyard" of other Princess Warriors and warriors alike—which produced fruit that multiplied in the knowledge of Jesus Christ, ready for harvest.

As Proverbs 31 Princess Warriors, Joanna, Susanna and Mary Magdalene fulfilled these verses:

> She considers a field and buys it; out of her earnings she plants a vineyard (v. 16).

> She opens her arms to the poor and extends her hands to the needy (v. 20).

Lydia

Lydia was recognized as a businesswoman. She was a purveyor of fine purple cloth—linen which was desired by the wealthy and dignitaries. She knew her business.

As a Proverbs 31 Princess Warrior, Lydia fulfilled these verses:

She sees that her trading is profitable, and her lamp does not go out at night (v. 18).

She makes coverings for her bed; she is clothed in fine linen and purple (v. 22).

She makes linen garments and sells them, and supplies the merchants with sashes (v. 24).

You

Princess Warrior, each one of these examples reflects other Proverbs 31 attributes, but my desire here is for us to focus on **our** gifts. When we compare ourselves to this passage in its entirety or to other Princess Warriors, we often feel inadequate, incapable and a failure. Instead, just like our examples, ask God to reveal your gifts and His plan. Use your gifts so that your works are praised. There is no one on this earth, whether in the past, present or future, that can do exactly what you can. No one can be *you*. Be the best *you* that *you* can be.

You may be a businessperson dealing in purple cloth, a missionary with a heart for the needy, a farmer who cultivates flax and wool, or a woman full of wisdom with a faithful tongue.

> Many women do noble things, but you surpass them all (v. 29).

Charm is deceptive, and beauty is fleeting; but a woman who fears the Lord is to be praised (v. 30).

Honor her for all that her hands have done, and let her works bring her praise at the city gate (v. 31).

No matter your gifts, embrace the Scriptures. Stop comparing. Bring honor to the warriors in your life and start living as the Proverbs 31 Princess Warrior God has called *you* to be.

You are fearfully and wonderfully made. You are significant in Christ. You will fight the good fight as a Princess Warrior for the Lord.

DISCUSSION

Princess Warrior, I hope you have become close to others in the group during this journey. Share your spiritual gifts and how you currently use those gifts. Ask your fellow Princess Warriors how they feel you already embody a Proverbs 31 Princess Warrior.

HOMEWORK

Next week is a celebration! Plan a celebration with your fellow Princess Warriors! Food, fun, worship, maybe meeting at a local restaurant. Whatever you decide as a group, your focus will be celebrating your victory as a Princess Warrior.

Do you know your spiritual gifts? When you have ten or fifteen minutes, go to spiritualgiftstest.com and take the test. Print the results and be prepared to share your spiritual gifts at the celebration.

WEEK 10

Conclusion And Celebration

Princess Warrior, what a journey! Together we have learned we are significant in Christ as Princess Warriors for the Lord! This week is simple. Share your spiritual gifts and celebrate!

As Christ followers, we each have different spiritual gifts. Together, we make up the body of Christ. With regard to our gifts, Paul writes in Romans:

For just as each of us has one body with many members, and these members do not all have the same function, so in Christ we, though many, form one body, and each member belongs to all the others. We have different gifts, according to the grace given to each of us. If your gift is prophesying, then prophesy in accordance with your faith; if it is serving, then serve; if it is teaching, then teach; if it is to encourage, then give encouragement; if it is giving, then give generously; if it is to lead, do it diligently; if it is to show mercy, do it cheerfully (Romans 12:4-8, NIV).

In 1 Corinthians, Paul lists the different gifts of the Spirit:

There are different kinds of gifts, but the same Spirit distributes them. There are different kinds of service, but the same Lord. There are different kinds of working, but in all of them and in everyone it is the same God at work. Now to each one the manifestation of the Spirit is given for the common good. To one there is given through the Spirit a message of *wisdom*, to another a message of *knowledge* by means of the same Spirit, to another *faith* by the same Spirit, to another gifts of *healing* by that one Spirit, to another *miraculous powers*, to another *prophecy*, to another *distinguishing between spirits*, to another *speaking in different kinds of tongues*, and to still another the *interpretation of tongues*. All these are the work of one and the same Spirit, and he distributes them to each one, just as he determines (1 Corinthians 12:4-11, NIV, emphasis added).

Upon completing your spiritual gifts test as part of your homework, you should have received your top three spiritual gifts. Take a moment to share and discuss these gifts with your fellow Princess Warriors. As you go through the group, recognize that it takes all of us to make up the full body of Christ!

Princess Warrior, I am so very proud of you! It is time now for you to live in the victory afforded you on the cross. Recognize you are significant in Christ! You no longer compare yourselves to others, but realize you have a place in God's army. Daily put on your armor, seek God's face and join the warriors and Princess Warriors in your brigade.

Recite:

I am fearfully and wonderfully made! I am significant in Christ!

I will fight the good fight as a Princess Warrior for the Lord!

I praise God for you and look forward to hearing your story in the days, months and years to come. Princess Warrior, celebrate!

Thank you for being a part of *Significance of a Princess Warrior*! Shalom!

Robyn S. Brinkley

CPSIA information can be obtained
at www.ICGtesting.com
Printed in the USA
FSOW01n0745050816
23474FS